TUNA AND SUSHI

Written by **Kimberly Bower**

Illustrated by **Nat Ellis**

A portion of this book's profits will be donated to San Diego's local TNR organization, Feral Cat Coalition. Thank you for helping the cats of San Diego and beyond.

Tuna and Sushi
Copyright © 2024 by Kimberly Bower

tunaandsushi.com

ISBN 979-8-218-50672-8 (paperback)
ISBN 979-8-218-50673-5 (hardcover)

Illustrated by Nat Ellis
Edited by Cara Stevens
Book design by Clarity DesignWorks

To my beloved community cats, Tuna and Sushi,
whose story inspired this book.

Tuna – my precious calendar boy.
May your sweet soul get all the pets your little heart desires.

Sushi – my charming and handsome little man.
May your whimsical spirit and wild way live on forever in this story.

I will love you both until the end of time.

To the unseen warriors in the shadows, Ivy and Mama Cat.
Your fierce beauty and strength will never be forgotten.

And to my girls, Nala and Sasha,
for always putting up with the stinky boy cats on the porch.

I'm Tuna.

This is my
brother, Sushi.

We live outside with our family in a small community called Castle Rock.

I've seen cats who live inside with people,
but Sushi and I prefer our outdoor home.

This neighborhood is all we've ever known.

Sushi is shy
around people and
likes to explore
on his own.

When I'm not hanging around with Sushi,
I stay close to home.

Sometimes we play,
and I chase after him.

Sometimes
we lie in the
sun, and he
tells me all about
his wild adventures.

Sometimes we visit
our wise friend, Ivy.

When we were kittens, Mama kept us safe. She showed us how to hide from predators and stay warm on chilly nights.

When we were old enough, we started to come
out and play. Mama stayed hidden but always
close by — just a howl and a hiss away.

Before long, Sushi and I discovered some curious people who live in our neighborhood. At first, we hid in the bushes and waited for them to leave.

But one day, they opened a can
of something that smelled so
good, I couldn't resist.

After that, our friends were bringing us food and water every night!
CLINK
CLINK
CLINK
KITTY FOOD

One friend, Miss Lady, even built us a special bed.

Every night, we heard the clinking of the cans...

And we knew it was time to eat!

Miss Lady started sitting closer while we ate. She smelled strange but had treats in her pocket — I was brave enough to eat one right from her hand!

One day, I brushed up against her leg, so she'd know I was ready for pets. Oh, did that feel PURR-fect!
But Sushi, not so much.
HISS!

Then one night,
Miss Lady took us away
in two separate crates.

"Where are we going?" I cried out.

I could see Sushi's wide-open eyes
through the bars of my crate.
Even Sushi was scared.

No wonder Mama told us to stay away from people!

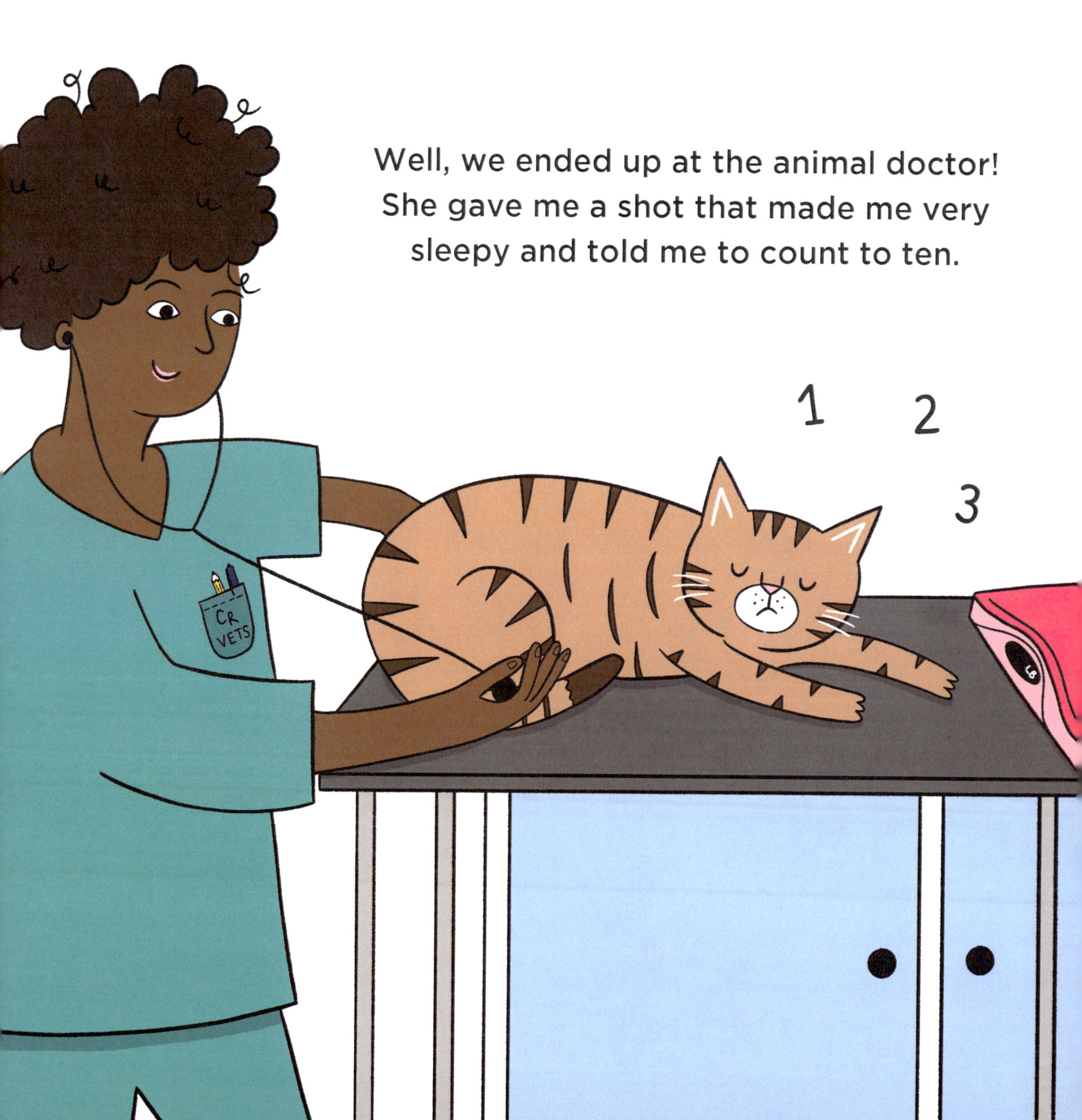

Well, we ended up at the animal doctor! She gave me a shot that made me very sleepy and told me to count to ten.
1
2
3
CR VETS

Then I woke up and it was already over!

After a long night stuck in that crate, I was
jolted awake by a shuffle. Something was
happening! I heard the crate open and
saw a flash of bright colors.

A familiar voice called out,
"Good boy, Tuna! Mama Cat is next!"

The bugs were buzzing, the birds were chirping,
and the air smelled fresh — I was HOME!

But wait, where was Sushi?

I looked for my brother high...

and low.

I saw a black cat who looked like Sushi, but his eyes were too blue.

And another cat who looked like Sushi, but her nose was too short.

There was another cat passing through, but he was WAY TOO STINKY!

I checked all our usual hiding spots,
but still no Sushi.

Just as I was about to give up,
a confident cat came strolling by.
"Sushi, is that you?" I chirped,
sniffing him out.

He smelled like Sushi and looked like Sushi.
But something was different, and I couldn't
put my whiskers on it.

"Yes, it's me. Who else would it be?"
Sushi cleaned his coat.
"What happened to your ear?"

I felt my ear and the tip was gone...just like Sushi's!
"You mean, what happened to OUR ears?
We'll have to ask Ivy about this!"

Just then, my stomach growled,
GRRRR

and we knew it was time for dinner.

That night, we waited until it was dark out for Ivy to make her rounds.

"Miss Lady took you to the veterinarian to keep you healthy and safe.

Your new ear-tips show everyone that
you are community cats who live outside
in the neighborhood."

"Like a crown of honor!" Sushi and I beamed.

Now, everyone in the community helps look after us. And we look after them, too.

Sushi is even staying closer
to home. He says we are
the kings of our castle.

And every night, we hear the clinking of the cans...

CLINK CLINK CLINK

And we know it is time to eat.

The End

COMMUNITY CAT FACTS

- **Community cat**: an unowned cat who lives outside. Community cats include feral and stray cats.
- **Feral cat**: a cat who has had little contact with people and is afraid or avoidant around them. Feral cats are usually happier living outside.
- **Stray cat**: a cat who is lost or has been abandoned. Stray cats can sometimes be adopted into homes.
- **Trap-Neuter-Return (TNR)**: the process of helping community cats by safely bringing them to a veterinarian for spay/neuter surgery, vaccines, an ear-tip, and then returning them to their outdoor homes. TNR helps cats, people, and the community!
- **Veterinarian**: a doctor who treats cats and other animals.
- **Spay/neuter**: when a veterinarian performs a surgery that prevents cats from having more kittens.
- **Ear-tip**: the universal sign that a community cat has been through TNR.
- **Caregiver**: a person who takes care of community cats. Caregivers bring community cats to the veterinarian for TNR and give them food, water, and shelter.

Did you know? Community cats can be feral, friendly, or anywhere in between.

tunaandsushi.com
Instagram: @tuna.n.sushi

By helping cats in need, you can be a hero in your own community!

A very special thanks to my family for all their extraordinary love and support.
You are the wind beneath my wings.

Thank you to GLW for helping me find my way (and my voice).
And thank you to DCB for encouraging me to dream big.

Another special thanks to Tuna's and Sushi's caregivers through the years,
and to all the caregivers, fosters, adopters, volunteers, staff, and veterinarians
who improve and save the lives of community cats. You are heroes.

Thank you to Nat Ellis for your brilliance and patience.

A portion of this book's profits will be donated to San Diego's
local TNR organization, Feral Cat Coalition. Thank you for helping
the cats of San Diego and beyond.

In loving memory of Emily Kilduff